Bodies of Water

Comparing Bodies of Water

Rebecca Rissman

Heinemann Library
Chicago, Illinois

www.heinemannraintree.com
Visit our website to find out
more information about
Heinemann-Raintree books.

To order:
☎ Phone 888-454-2279
💻 Visit www.heinemannraintree.com
to browse our catalog and order online.

©2010 Heinemann Library
an imprint of Capstone Global Library, LLC
Chicago, Illinois

Edited by Rebecca Rissman, Siân Smith, and Charlotte Guillain
Designed by Kimberly Miracle and Joanne Malivoire
Picture research by Elizabeth Alexander
Originated by Capstone Global Library
Printed and bound in China by Leo Paper Products Ltd

14 13 12 11 10
10 9 8 7 6 5 4 3 2 1

Library of Congress Cataloging-in-Publication Data
Rissman, Rebecca.
    Comparing bodies of water / Rebecca Rissman.
        p. cm.
    Includes bibliographical references and index.
    ISBN 978-1-4329-3341-8 (hc) -- ISBN 978-1-4329-3342-5
(pb) 1. Bodies of water--Juvenile literature. I. Title.
    GB662.3.R57 2008
    551.46--dc22
                                        2008055663

Acknowledgments
The author and publishers are grateful to the following for
permission to reproduce copyright material:
Alamy pp. **10** (© BAE Inc), **19 left** (© Reinhard Dirscherl),
21 right (© blickwinkel); Corbis pp. **5** (© Frans Lanting),
12 (© Ashley Cooper), **13** (© Grafton Smith), **14** (© Blaine
Harrington III), **16** (© Larry Mulvehill), **20 right** (© Theo
Allofs); Getty Images p. **7** (Altrendo Images); Photolibrary pp.
6 (Christian Kober/Robert Harding Travel), **7** (Mark Deeble
& Victoria Stone/Oxford Scientific), **8** (Seux Paule/Hemis), **9**
(David B Fleetham/Oxford Scientific), **15** (Elliott Neep/Oxford
Scientific), **18 left** (David B Fleetham/Oxford Scientific), **18
right** (Oxford Scientific), **19 right** (Tony Bomford/Oxford
Scientific), **20 left** (Ralph A Clevenger/Flirt Collection), **21 left**
(Rick Sherwin); Shutterstock pp. **4** (© Thorsten Rust), **11** (©
AridOcean), **17** (© Christopher Elwell).

Front cover photograph of a river delta with the sea in the
background reproduced with permission of Shutterstock/ ©
Digitalife.

Back cover photograph of lakes and ponds reproduced with
permission of Corbis/© Blaine Harrington III.

We would like to thank Nancy Harris and Adriana Scalise for
their help in the preparation of this book.

Every effort has been made to contact copyright holders of
any material reproduced in this book. Any omissions will
be rectified in subsequent printings if notice is given to the
publisher.

Some words are shown in bold, **like this.** They are
explained in "Words to Know" on page 23.

Contents

About this series

Books in the **Bodies of Water** series introduce readers to the different types of bodies of water. Use this book to stimulate discussion about the differences between lakes, ponds, oceans, seas, rivers, streams, and canals. Also encourage children to think about the animals and plants that live in different bodies of water.

Water on Earth

Pictures of planet Earth always look blue. This is because most of Earth is covered with water. An area of water is called a body of water.

There are many types of bodies of water. Bodies of water can be very big. And bodies of water can be small, too.

Fresh Water

Bodies of water can be made of **fresh water**. Fresh water is not salty.

turtle

Humans drink fresh water. Humans also wash with fresh water. Animals and plants need fresh water to live. Many different animals live in fresh water.

Salt Water

salt

Bodies of water can be made of salt water. Salt water tastes salty.

Humans do not drink salt water. Many different animals and plants live in salt water.

Oceans and Seas

Oceans are the largest bodies of water on Earth. A **sea** is a smaller body of water. Most seas are smaller parts of oceans. Oceans and seas are made of salt water.

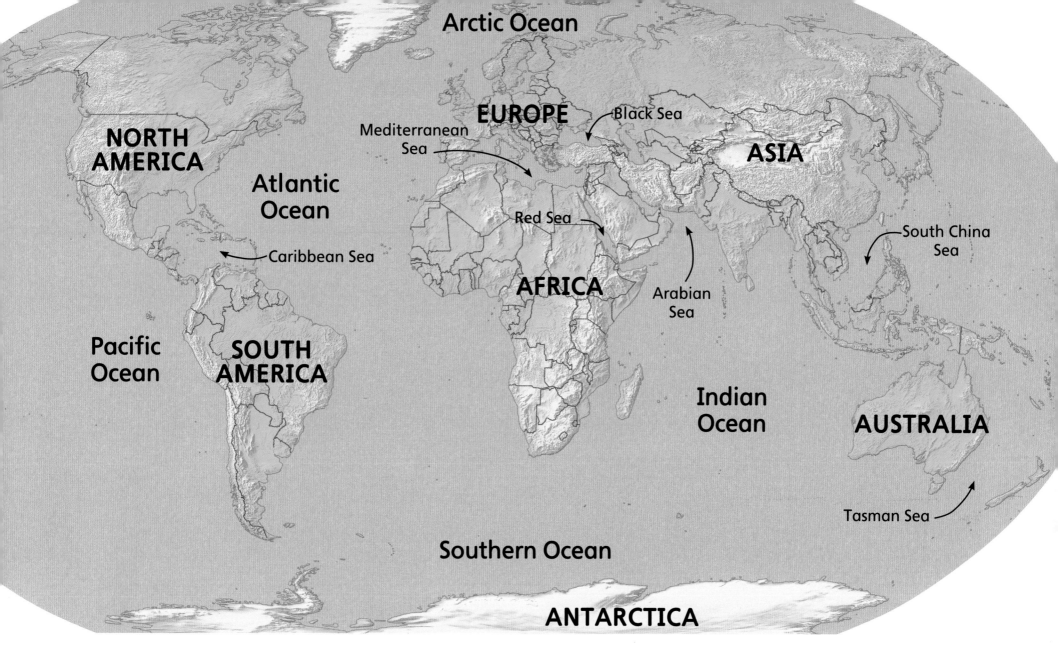

There are five oceans. Oceans are divided by seven **continents**, or large pieces of land. There are many seas.

Rivers and Streams

A **river** is water that flows across the land.
A **stream** is a small river. Rivers and streams are
made of **fresh water**.

Rivers and streams are formed from rain water or melting snow. Rivers and streams can **erode**, or wash away soil and rock, to form **valleys**.

Lakes and Ponds

Lakes are large areas of land covered by water. Lakes are **surrounded** by land. **Ponds** are very small lakes. Most lakes and ponds are made of **fresh water**.

Lakes and ponds are in low areas of land. Water from snow and rain settles in lakes and ponds. The land around lakes and ponds is higher.

Canals

Canals are waterways that connect two bodies of water. Canals can connect **oceans**. Canals can connect **rivers**. Canals can connect **lakes**.

Canals are made by humans. Canals are like roads. Boats use canals to get to places quickly.

Water Life

Bodies of water are home to many types of animals. Some whales live in **oceans**. Some fish live in **rivers**.

Some giant tortoises live in **seas**. Some shellfish live in **lakes**.

Bodies of water are home to many types of plants. Sea kelp lives in some **seas**. Water lilies live in some **ponds**.

Mangrove trees live at the shores of some **oceans**.
Seaweed lives in some **lakes** and ponds.

Saving Water

Water is a **natural resource**. Natural resources are things we use that come from Earth. We need to be careful with natural resources and not use too much of them.

We can use less water when we:
+ take a shower instead of a bath
+ turn off the tap when we brush our teeth
+ use a watering can in the garden instead of a hose

Words to Know

canal	water pathway that connects two bodies of water. Canals are made by people.
continent	large area of land. The land on Earth is divided into seven continents.
erode	wear away
fresh water	water that is not salty like sea water
lake	large area of water on land. Lakes have land all around them.
natural resource	things we use that exist naturally in the world. Water and trees are natural resources.
ocean	one of the large bodies of salt water that cover most of the Earth. There are five oceans on Earth.
pond	small area of land covered by water. Ponds are like small lakes.
river	water that flows across the land
sea	small part of an ocean
stream	small river
surround	cover something on all sides
valley	low area of land with high sides

Index

Note to Parents and Teachers

Before Reading:

Show children a map of the world or a globe. Ask children why parts of Earth are blue. Explain to children that the blue parts show bodies of water. Together, begin creating a chart entitled "Bodies of Water." Write the following titles to create three columns: "What You Know," "What You Want to Know," and "What You've Learned." Discuss the first two columns with the children and then fill them in.

After Reading:

Continue discussing and filling in the chart with the children. Focus on the third column: "What You've Learned." Ask children what they learned from this book. After children have listed their ideas, discuss how they can save water by taking showers instead of baths, using a watering can instead of a hose, and making sure taps are turned off. Ask the children to create signs that show different ways to save water.